Simply Beethoven

The Music of Ludwig van Beethoven
27 of His Timeless Masterpieces
Arranged by Jerry Ray

Simply Beethoven is a collection of the most famous compositions by Ludwig van Beethoven (1770–1827), highlighting some of his most successful genres—piano sonatas, symphonies, overtures and more. These pieces have been carefully selected and arranged by Jerry Ray for Easy Piano, making many of Beethoven's most inspired works accessible to pianists of all ages. Phrase markings, articulations, fingering and dynamics have been included to aid with interpretation, and a large print size makes the notation easy to read.

Ludwig van Beethoven lived at the turn of the 19th century, and many consider him the bridge between the Classical and Romantic periods of music history. His compositions often inspired nicknames: the "Emperor" concerto, the "Moonlight" sonata, "Rage Over the Lost Penny," and the "Eroica" symphony, to name a few. While Mozart's music is known for balance, clarity and logic, Beethoven's music contains sudden bursts of excitement, surprising key changes, and experimental use of form. Beethoven also helped expand keyboard technique, which paved the way for Czerny, Liszt, and the other virtuosos of the Romantic period and beyond. For these reasons and many more, his compositions are exciting to explore.

After all, he is *Simply Beethoven!*

Contents

Bagatelle, Op. 33, No. 6

Ludwig van Beethoven
Arranged by Jerry Ray

4

5

Ecossaise, WoO 83

Ludwig van Beethoven
Arranged by Jerry Ray

Animato

Ecossaise in G Major, WoO 23

Ludwig van Beethoven
Arranged by Jerry Ray

Allegro

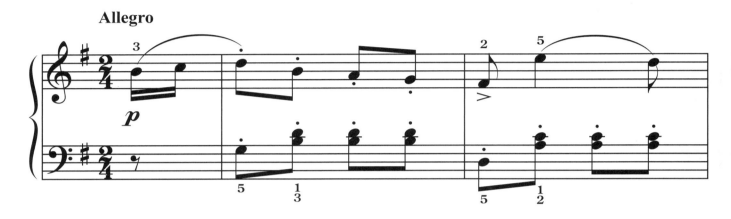

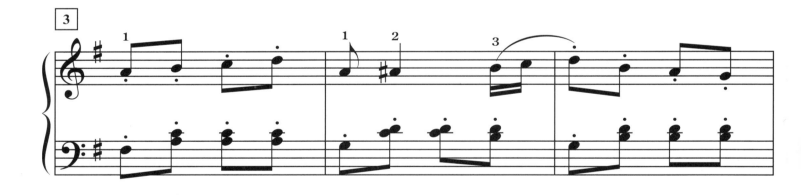

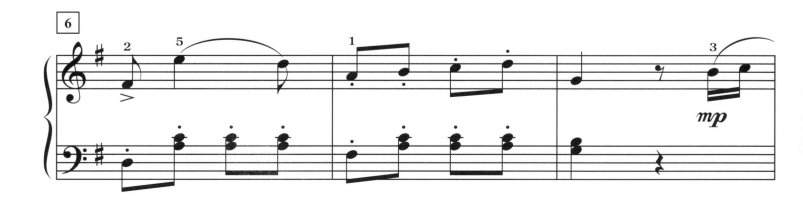

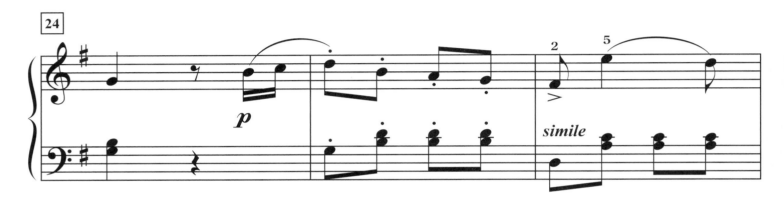

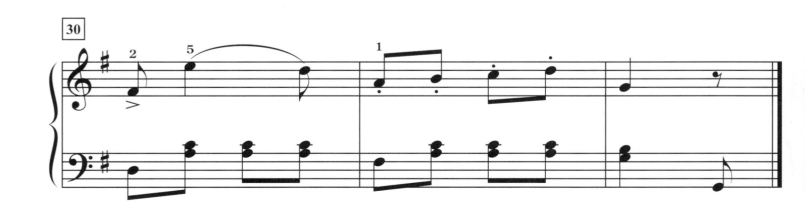

Egmont Overture, Op. 84
(Theme)

Ludwig van Beethoven
Arranged by Jerry Ray

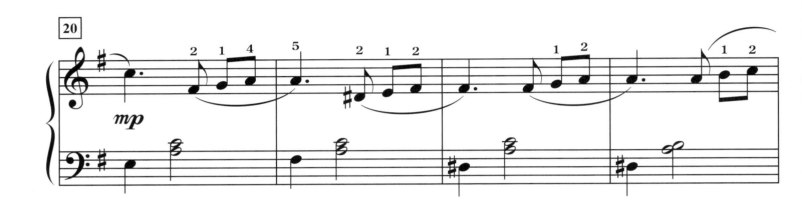

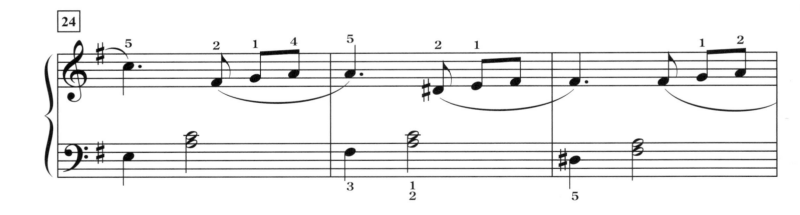

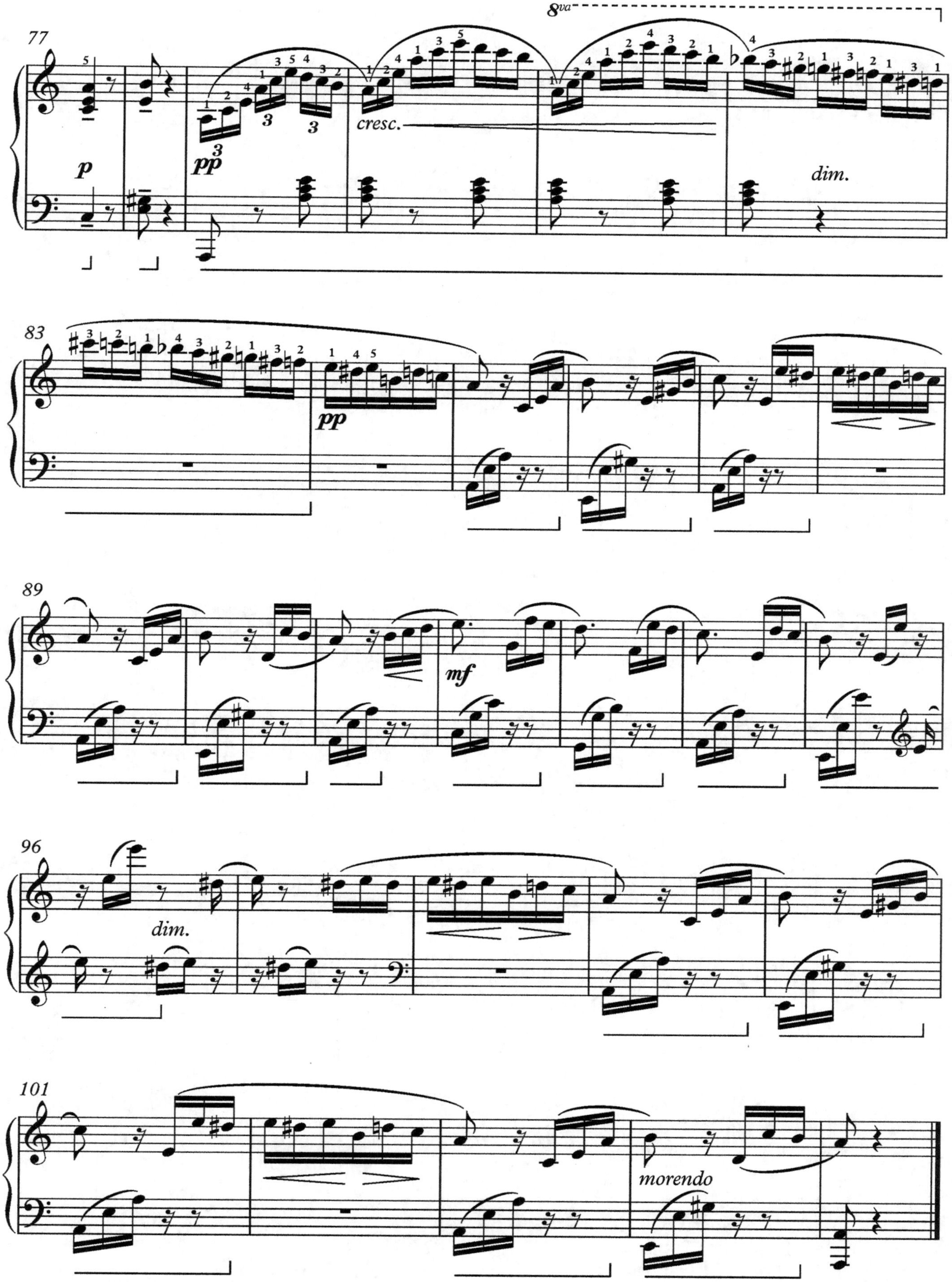
77
8va
p
pp
cresc.
dim.
83
pp
89
mf
96
dim.
101
morendo

Für Elise

Ludwig van Beethoven
Arranged by Jerry Ray

Moderato

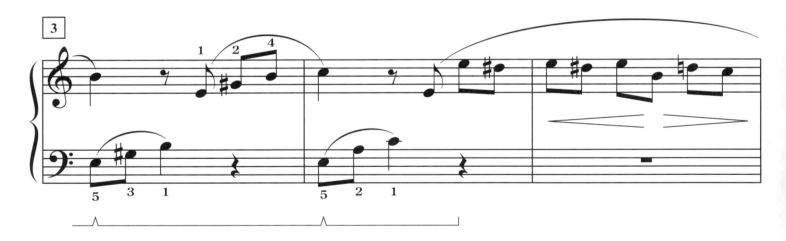

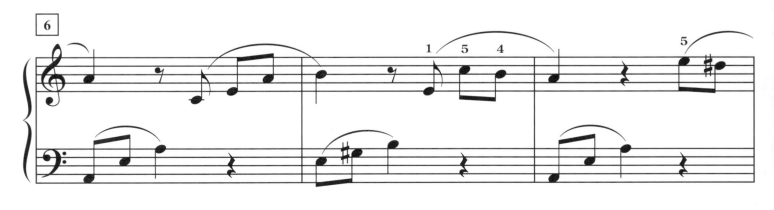

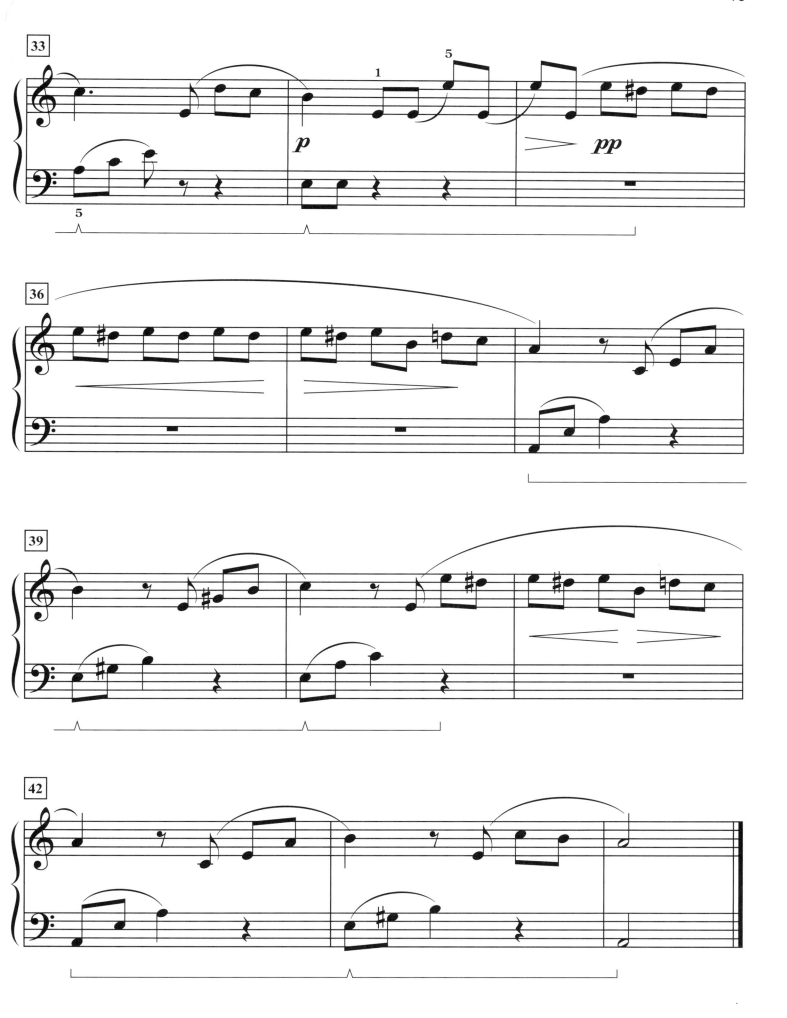

German Dance, WoO 42, No. 6

Ludwig van Beethoven
Arranged by Jerry Ray

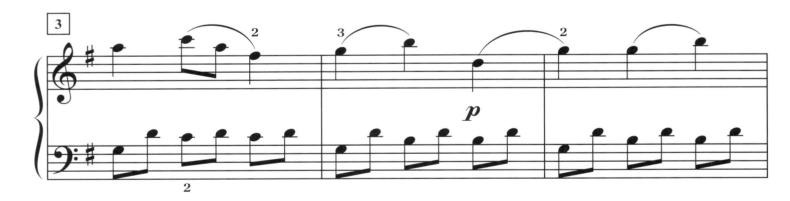

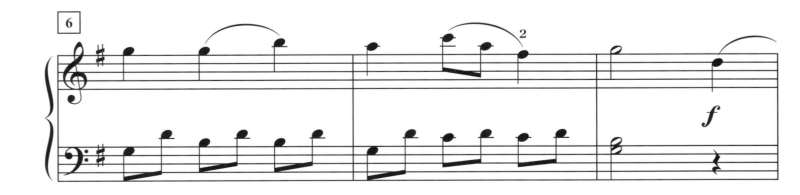

German Dance, WoO 42, No. 3

(Trio Theme)

Ludwig van Beethoven
Arranged by Jerry Ray

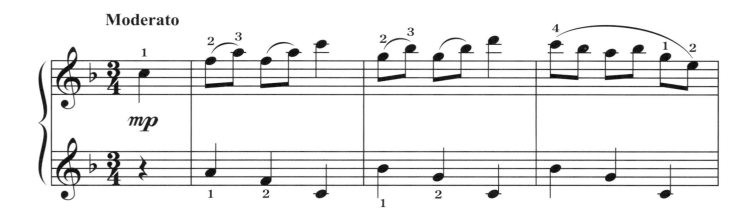

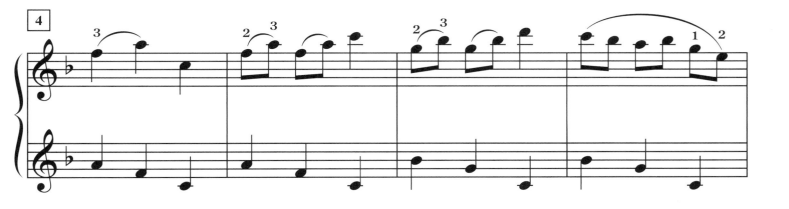

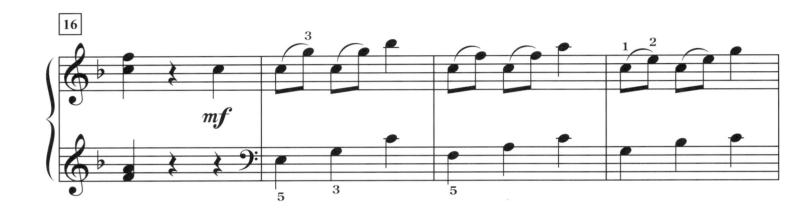

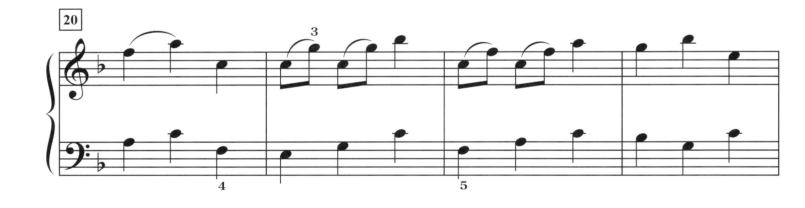

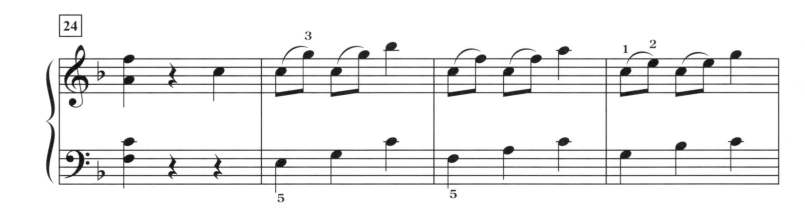

Bagatelle in A Minor, Op. 119, No. 9

Ludwig van Beethoven
Arranged by Jerry Ray

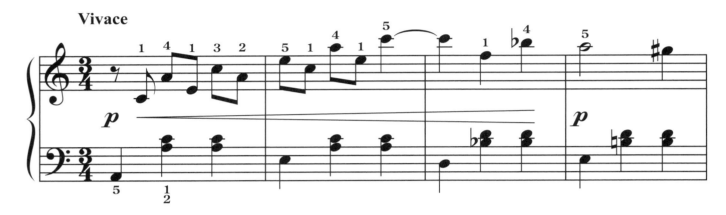

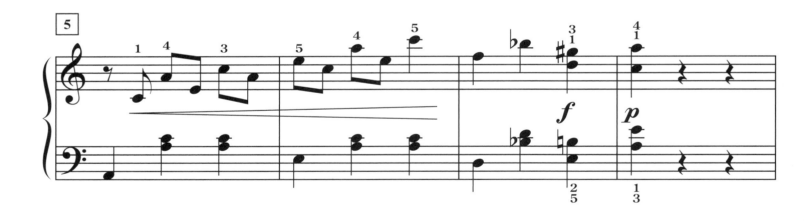

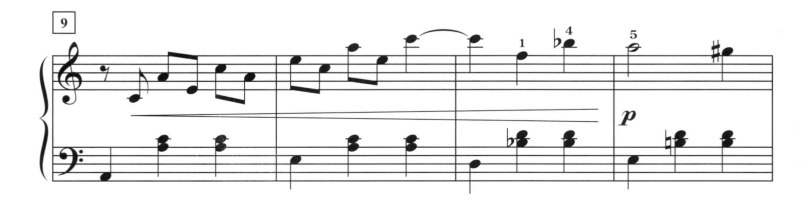

Minuet in G

Ludwig van Beethoven
Arranged by Jerry Ray

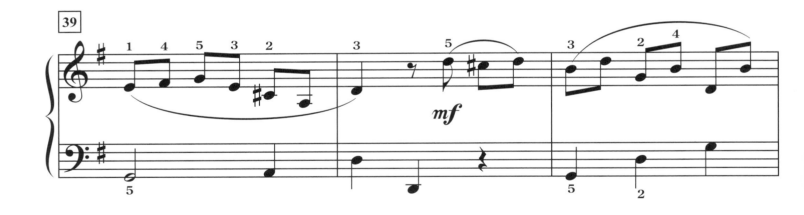

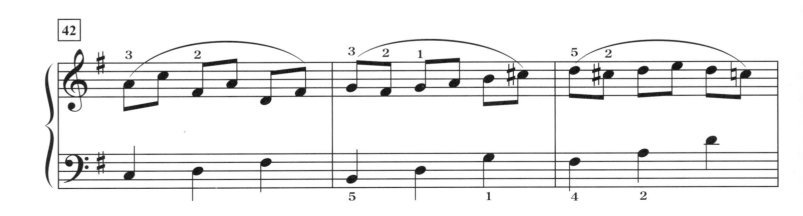

Piano Concerto No. 3

(First Movement Theme)

Ludwig van Beethoven
Arranged by Jerry Ray

Piano Concerto No. 3

(Third Movement Theme)

Ludwig van Beethoven
Arranged by Jerry Ray

Piano Sonata No. 8 in C Minor, Op. 13 ("Pathétique")

(Second Movement)

Ludwig van Beethoven
Arranged by Jerry Ray

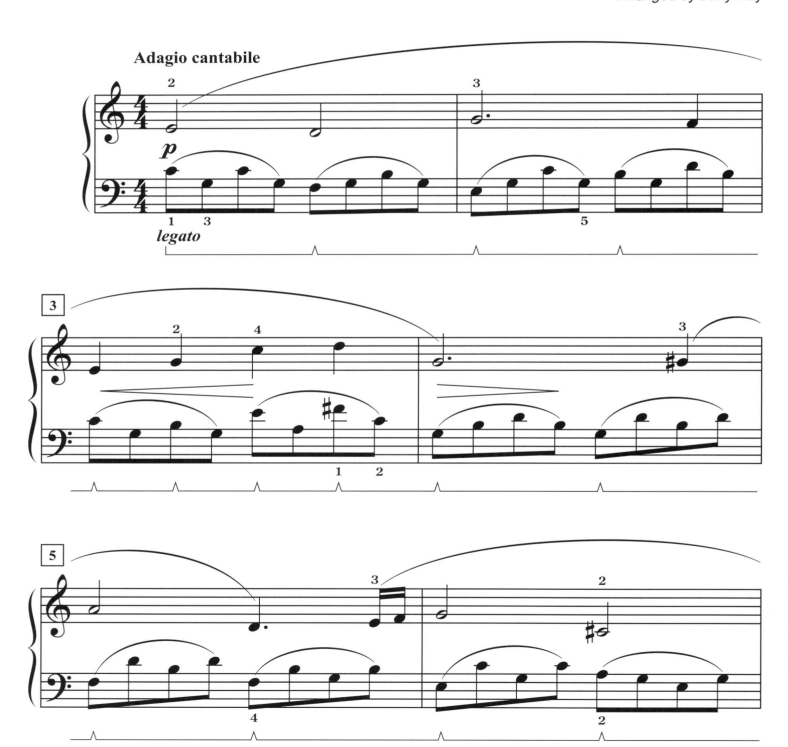

Piano Sonata No. 8 in C Minor, Op. 13
("Pathétique")

(Third Movement)

Ludwig van Beethoven
Arranged by Jerry Ray

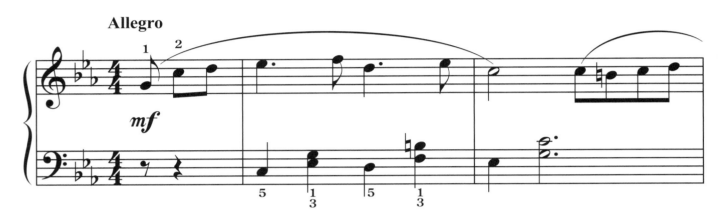

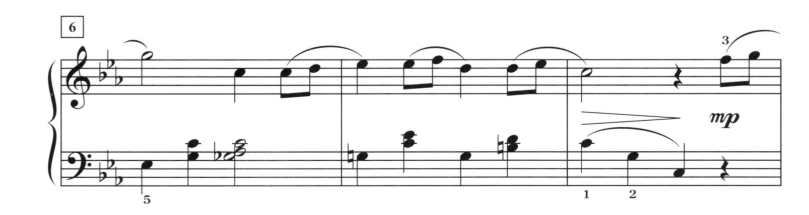

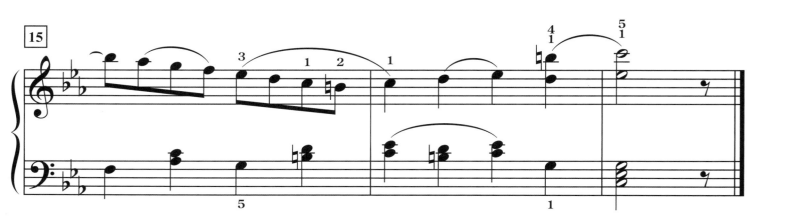

Piano Sonata No. 14 in C-sharp Minor, Op. 27, No. 2 ("Moonlight")

(First Movement)

Ludwig van Beethoven
Arranged by Jerry Ray

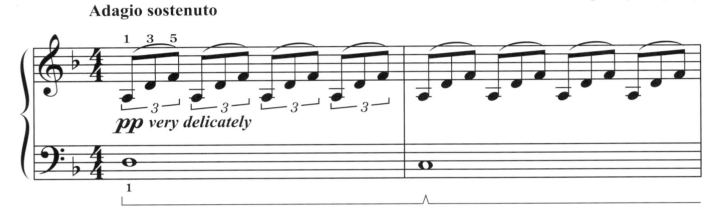

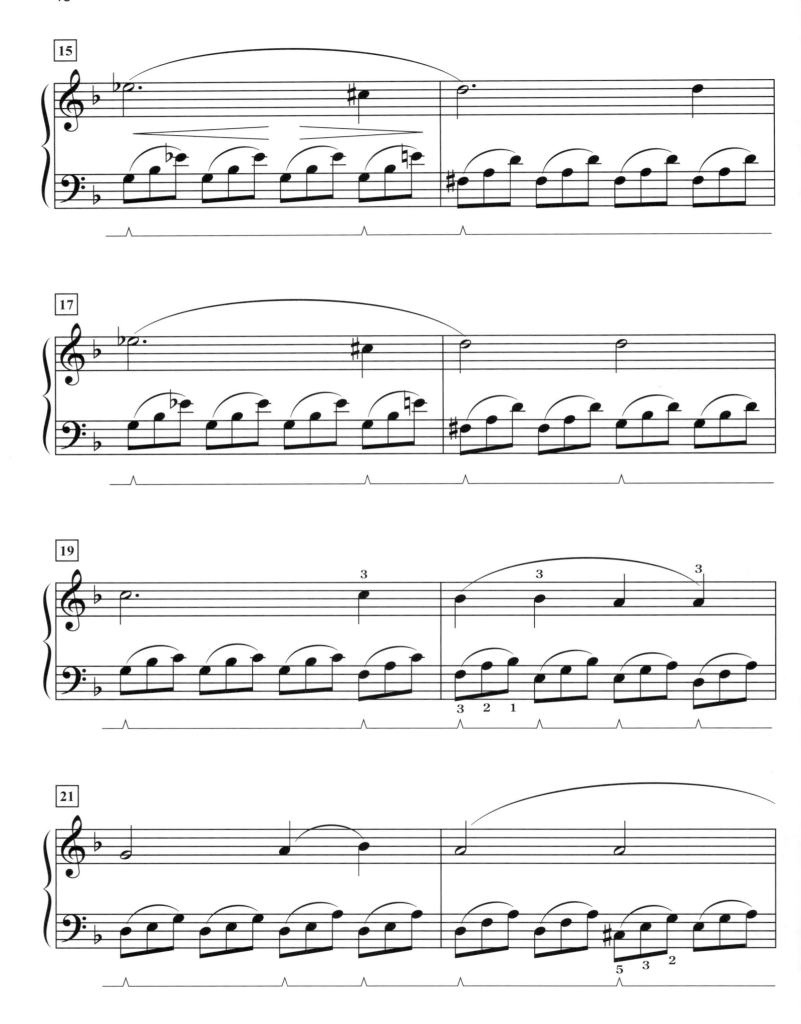

Piano Sonata No. 15 in D Major, Op. 28 ("Pastoral")

Ludwig van Beethoven
Arranged by Jerry Ray

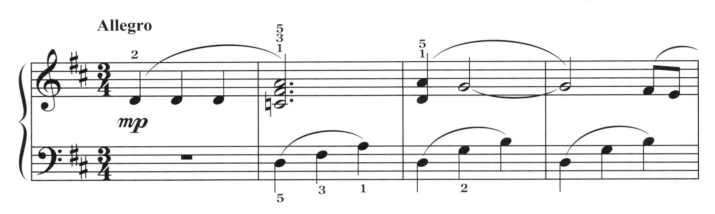

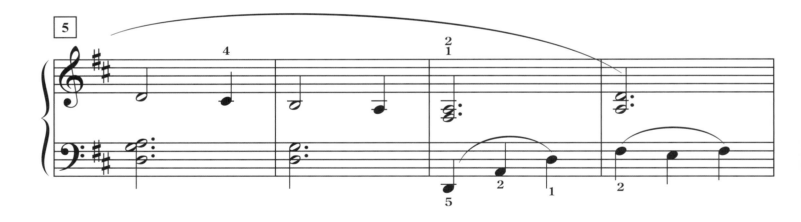

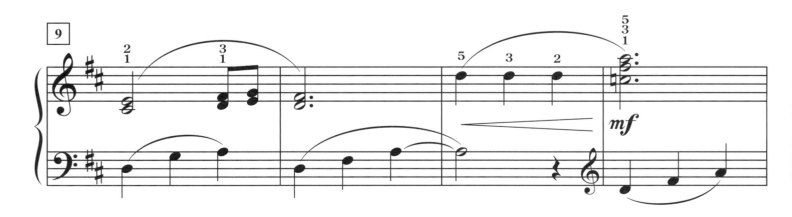

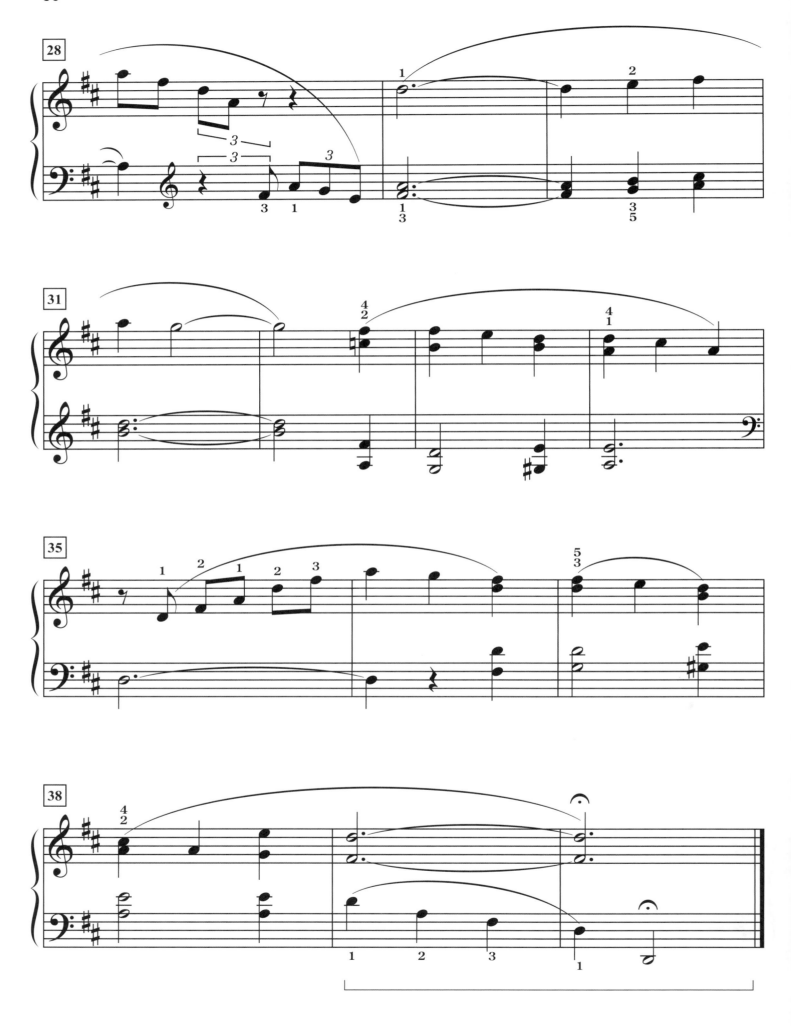

Piano Sonata No. 19 in G Minor, Op. 49, No. 1

(Second Movement)

Ludwig van Beethoven
Arranged by Jerry Ray

Piano Sonata No. 20, Op. 49, No. 2

(Second Movement)
(originally in the key of G Major)

Ludwig van Beethoven
Arranged by Jerry Ray

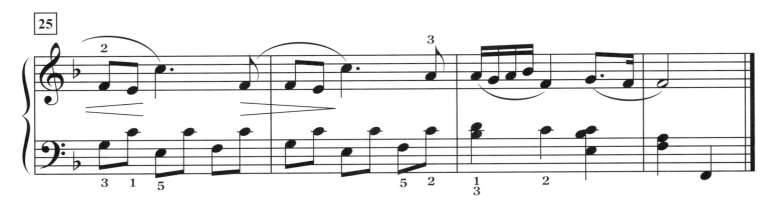

Rondo a capriccio, Op. 129

("Rage Over the Lost Penny")

Ludwig van Beethoven
Arranged by Jerry Ray

Sonatina in G Major

Ludwig van Beethoven
Arranged by Jerry Ray

Moderato

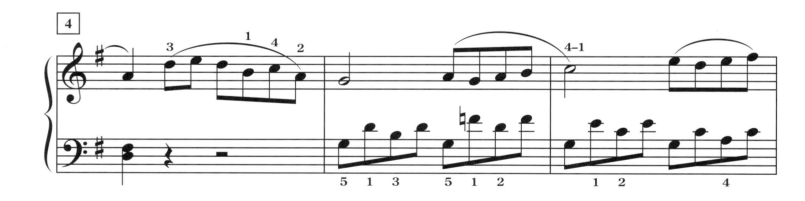

58

Symphony No. 1
(Fourth Movement Theme)

Ludwig van Beethoven
Arranged by Jerry Ray

61

Symphony No. 3 ("Eroica")

(Fourth Movement Theme)

Ludwig van Beethoven
Arranged by Jerry Ray

Allegretto

Symphony No. 5

(First Movement Theme)

Ludwig van Beethoven
Arranged by Jerry Ray

Allegro con brio

Piano Concerto No. 5 ("Emperor")

(Second Movement Theme)

Ludwig van Beethoven
Arranged by Jerry Ray

Adagio un poco mosso

Symphony No. 7
(Second Movement Theme)

Ludwig van Beethoven
Arranged by Jerry Ray

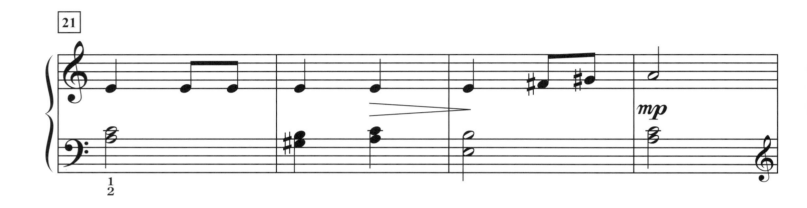

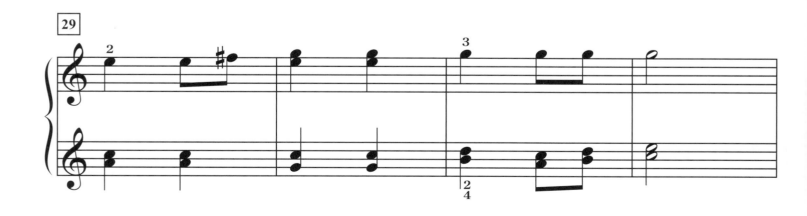

Symphony No. 9 ("Ode to Joy")

(Fourth Movement Theme)

Ludwig van Beethoven
Arranged by Jerry Ray

Allegro maestoso

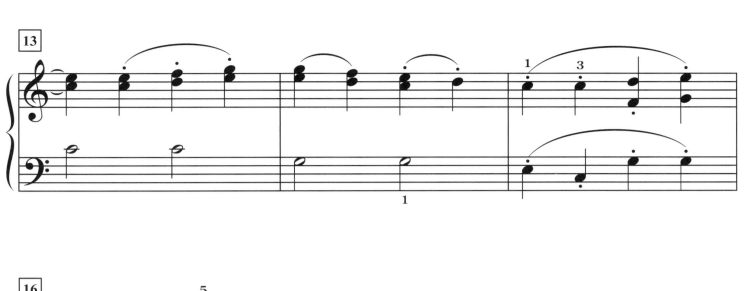

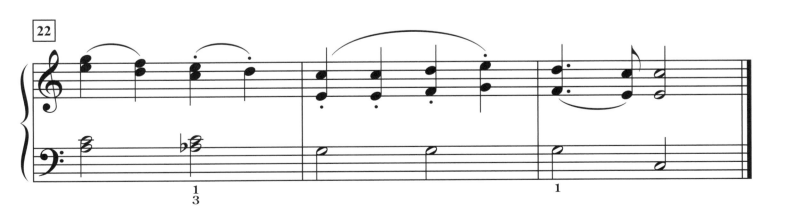

Variation on the Paisiello duet
"Nel cor piu non mi sento"

Ludwig van Beethoven
Arranged by Jerry Ray

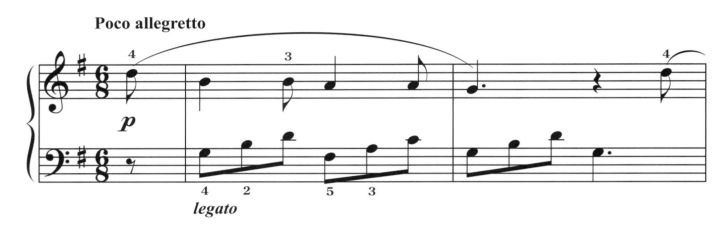

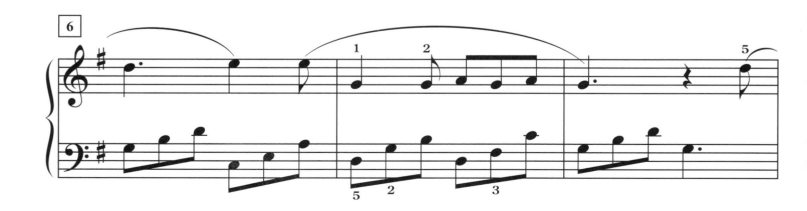

Turkish March

(from *The Ruins of Athens*)

Ludwig van Beethoven
Arranged by Jerry Ray

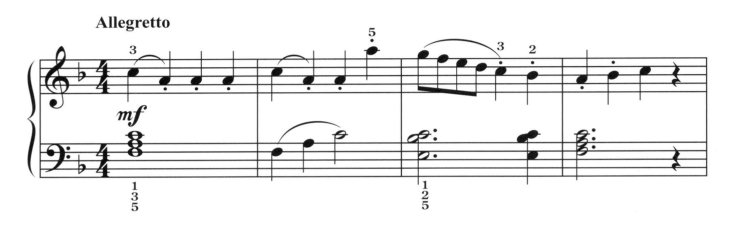

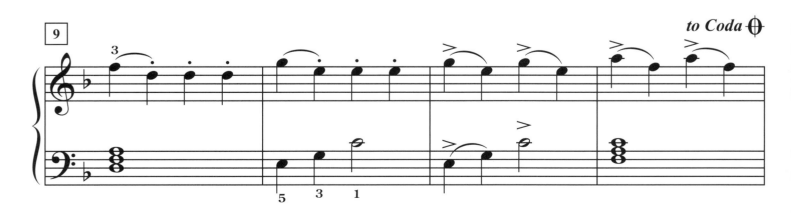

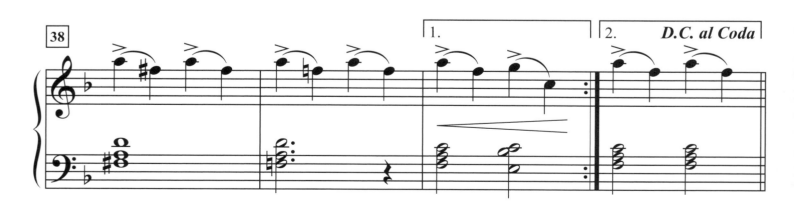

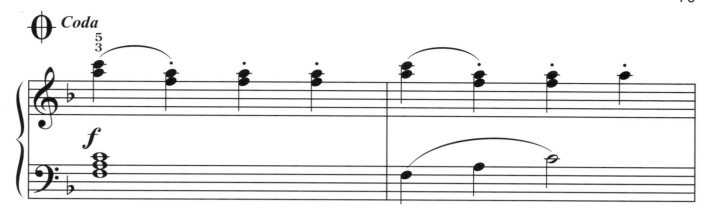

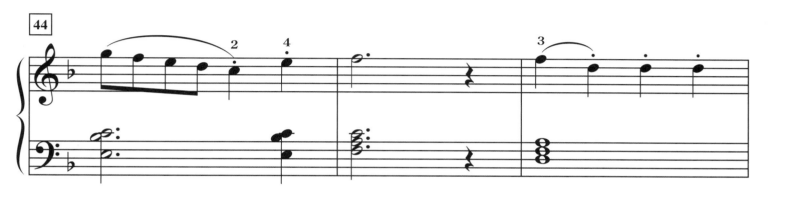

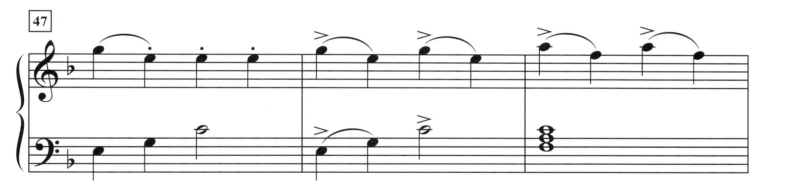

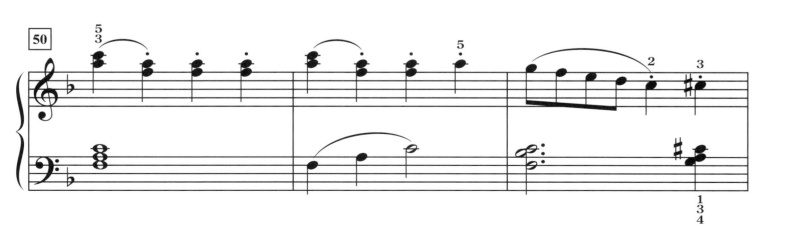

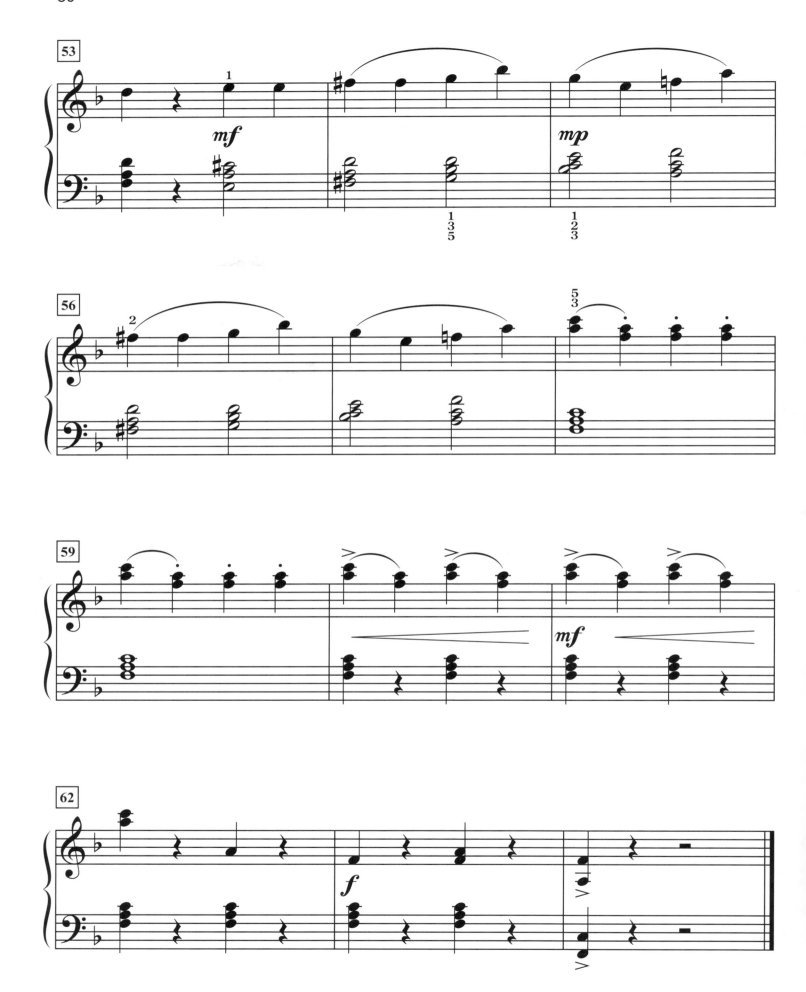